LOST AND FOUND

THE TERRACOTTA ARMY
AND OTHER
Lost Treasures

JOHN MALAM

QEB Publishing

Copyright © QEB Publishing, Inc. 2011

Published in the United States by
QEB Publishing, Inc.
3 Wrigley, Suite A
Irvine, CA 92618

www.qed-publishing.co.uk

ISBN 978 1 60992 052 4

Printed in China

Project Editor Carey Scott
Designer Stefan Morris Design
Illustrations The Art Agency
and MW Digital Graphics
Picture Researcher Maria Joannou

Front cover image: Terracotta figures from
the Qin army vaults, southwest China

Library of Congress Cataloging-in-Publication Data
Malam, John, 1957-
Terracotta Army and other lost treasures / John Malam.
    p. cm. -- (Lost and found)
    Summary: "Describes the historical circumstances that led to treasures such as the Terracotta
Army and the Dead Sea Scrolls being lost or hidden and the archaeological discoveries that found
evidence of these treasures"--Provided by publisher.
    Includes index.
    ISBN 978-1-60992-052-4 (library bound : alk. paper)
    1. Antiquities--Juvenile literature. 2. Treasure troves--History--
Juvenile literature. 3. Civilization, Ancient--Juvenile literature.
    I. Title.
    CC171.M35 2012
    930.1--dc22
                                            2011012121

Picture credits

AKG-Images Erich Lessing 16bl, 17br; The Art Gallery Collection 16-17, 30; The Art Agency Ian Jackson 10b,
14b, 18b, 23b, 27b; Bridgeman Art Library Giraudon 25b, Boltin Picture Library 27t, 31c; Corbis Eddie Keogh/
Reuters 2br, 5, Paul Souders 8t, Nathan Benn/Ottochrome 13t, Jason Hawkes 15b, Jim Hollander/EPA 21br,
Mimmo Jodice 22b, Adam Woolfitt 26b, Bettmann 29b, Mimmo Jodice 31b; DK Images Richard Bonson 6b;
Getty Images AFP Photo/Nikolay Doychinov 4bl, National Geographic/O. Louis Mazzatenta 7b, ChinaFotoPress
8-9b, AFP/Norbert Millauer 9t, Time & Life Pictures 12t, Popperfoto 12b, AFP/Menahem Kahana 20bl, National
Geographic 20-21, AFP/Mario Laporta 23t, Roger Viollet 24br, AFP Photo/Nikolay Doychinov 31t; Photolibrary
Michael Krabs 7t; Photoshot World Illustrated 29t; The Picture Desk Art Archive/Musée du Louvre Paris/Gianni
Dagli Orti 2tr, 11t, 24t, 24bl, 25t, 25c; Rex Features Alinari 4tr; Shutterstock Holbox 1t, Leungchopan 1l, Hung
Chung Chih 1br, Denisart 8-9 (background), Alfredo Ragazzoni 11b Kzww 16-17 (background), Denisart 20-
21 (background), Ella's Design 19t; The Trustees of the British Museum British Museum Images 15t; Topham
Picturepoint 9b, 28-29b, The Granger Collection 3, The British Library 6tl, RIA Novosti 13b, The Granger
Collection 19b, 28t. All maps by Mark Walker at MW Digital Graphics 6tr, 14t, 18t, 22t, 26t

The words in **bold** are explained in the Glossary on page 31.

CONTENTS

WHAT IS TREASURE?

Whether it's a hoard of ancient gold and silver or a collection of dusty old scrolls, there is something magical about treasure. It has its own story to tell, opening up windows on the past.

Perhaps the owners of the treasure lived in troubled times, and hid their most valuable possessions somewhere safe, but were never able to recover them. Some treasures were lost by accident, such as when ships loaded with valuable cargoes sank without a trace. Other treasures were intended to stay hidden for ever, buried in graves out of the reach of thieves and **treasure hunters**. For as long as a treasure stays hidden, its story remains a secret.

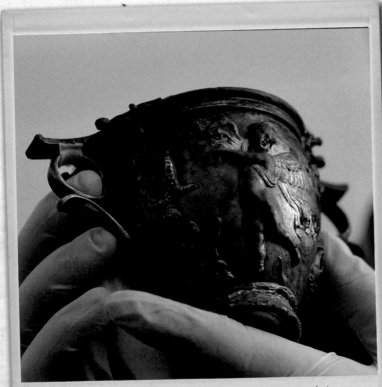

▲ In 2009, treasure hunters damaged an ancient tomb in Bulgaria. Archeologists went to investigate, and they unearthed this rare silver cup, decorated with figures from Greek mythology. They think it is about 2,000 years old.

▲ This **bronze** statue of a warrior was made in ancient Greece in about 450 BCE. It was being taken to Italy, but the ship carrying it sank. It was found on the seabed by a diver in 1972.

But when a long-lost treasure is found, people ask questions about it. How old is it? Who put it there and why? We want to know about the people who lost the treasure and the world in which they lived. The answers to our questions are not always easy to discover, but there are clues in the treasure that **archeologists** and other experts can find. So the loss of the treasure hundreds or thousands of years ago is, today, our good fortune.

The Staffordshire Hoard

In Staffordshire, England, on July 5, 2009, an amateur treasure hunter with a metal detector made an incredible find: pieces of gold from swords and crosses, and parts of helmets. Archeologists were called in. Soon they had uncovered more than 1,500 gold and silver items buried in the 7th century CE, the largest hoard of Anglo-Saxon treasure ever found. Experts do not know why the Staffordshire Hoard, as the treasure became known, was buried. Some say it was a collection of trophies looted after a battle.

▲ Objects from the the Staffordshire Hoard, probably pieces from hilts and other sword parts that could be attached to sword blades and reused.

LOST:
ALL THE EMPEROR'S MEN

Location: Near Xi'an, eastern China
Date: 210 BCE

The first emperor of China, Qin Shi Huang, was the most powerful person in the world. He controlled all of China and its millions of people. To protect his vast empire he built the Great Wall of China, the largest single structure on Earth.

But Emperor Qin wanted more than this—he wanted to live forever. He searched for the secret of immortality, and his doctors gave him **mercury** medicine which they said would prolong his life. In fact, it slowly poisoned him, and he died in 210 BCE aged 50. Years before his death, Emperor Qin had chosen the place he was to be buried. For 40 years, 700,000 men worked to prepare an incredible underground tomb for him, where it was believed he would be able to realize his dream of eternal life. According to an ancient writer, the tomb was made of bronze and on its floor was a map of China with rivers of mercury. As long as the mercury rivers flowed, Emperor Qin would continue to live in a world below the ground.

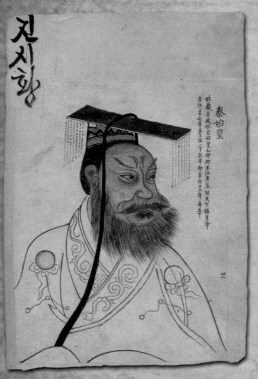

▲ Qin Shi Huang became ruler of Qin state when he was just 13 years old. He conquered all the other independent kingdoms to become the first emperor of the whole of China.

▲ The life-size warriors stood in row upon row. Their backs were to the Emperor, so that they were ready to face the enemy and protect their leader for all eternity.

The Emperor's tomb was surrounded by more than 600 pits containing everything he would need for eternal life—chariots and horses, armor and helmets, pottery figures of acrobats, dancers, musicians, and officials, and even rare birds and animals. The three biggest pits contained the Emperor's army—a fighting force of more than 8,000 armed men and horses made from baked clay, called **terracotta**.

◀ Thousands of unpaid laborers worked to build the Emperor's tomb. It was designed as a palace for him to live out eternal life, and it contained many different buildings including offices and halls.

Model Warriors

Every terracotta warrior was unique: each had different features or expressions. Some of them may have been modeled on real soldiers from Emperor Qin's army. Craftspeople fixed the ears, noses, and hair in place, and sculpted the mouths, eyes, beards, and mustaches straight onto the heads.

FOUND:
THE TERRACOTTA ARMY

In March 1974, farmers in Shaanxi province needed more water for their crops. They began drilling wells, but instead of water the farmers found pieces of broken pottery and fragments of bronze weapons. They looked old. What were they, and what were they doing there?

Soon, one of the greatest discoveries in the history of archeology was being made. Buried deep beneath the fields, in massive pits, was an army of pottery figures. It soon became known around the world as the Terracotta Army. For 2,200 years, it had guarded Emperor Qin's **burial mound**. Only the ravages of time had troubled the warriors.

The roofs that once covered the pits had collapsed long before, knocking the figures over and smashing them to pieces. The pits filled up with earth, burying the broken warriors. Their colorful paintwork faded and flaked. But piece by piece, archeologists are putting the figures back together to reveal the true might of Emperor Qin's army.

▲ As earth is cleared away, the smashed remains of the incredible Terracotta Army come to light—for now just a jigsaw of broken brown pottery.

▶ Archeologists excavate a terracotta warrior from No.1 pit. By 2010, only about 1,000 of the estimated 8,000 existing figures had been excavated.

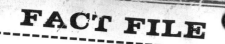

FACT FILE

Each warrior took about 150 days to make, from shaping and firing the clay to painting the finished figure.

▲ The terracotta warriors were originally painted in bright colors. Art restorers are studying the composition of the paints used so they can eventually recreate them.

The Emperor's Tomb

About a mile (1.5 kilometers) from the site of the Terracotta Army is the burial mound of Emperor Qin. It is covered by a huge artificial hill. The Emperor is buried deep inside, perhaps surrounded by rivers of flowing mercury. Archeologists are not yet ready to explore the tomb, but they have probed the soil and found traces of mercury, just as an ancient writer said. No one knows what treasures might be inside the tomb, but one day we will find out.

9

FOUND:
THE GOLD OF TROY

Homer was a storyteller in ancient Greece. He wrote a famous story called *The Iliad* which described the city of Troy. As the centuries passed, *The Iliad* came to be seen as a myth—a made-up story. But in the nineteenth century, a German schoolboy became convinced that Homer's story was fact not fiction, and the city of Troy had really existed.

His name was Heinrich Schliemann, and he dreamed of finding Troy. Schliemann became a wealthy banker and, in the 1860s, he began searching for the city he believed had once existed. He traveled to Turkey, and when he came to a huge mound known as Hissarlik, which means Place of Fortresses, he was sure he had found the site of ancient Troy.

▲ In 1874, Sophia Schliemann was photographed wearing the golden diadem (headband) and necklace found by her husband at Troy. The headband was made from 16,000 pieces of gold threaded onto gold wire.

Lost Again

The Trojan treasure was on display in a museum in Berlin, Germany, from 1881 to 1941. During the Second World War, German museum staff moved it to a bombproof tower for safekeeping. But in 1945 the Russian army entered Berlin (right), and the treasure disappeared. For many years its whereabouts were a mystery. In 1993 the Russians admitted they had the treasure, and today it is displayed in Moscow's Pushkin Museum.

In 1870, Schliemann paid local workers to dig into the hill of Hissarlik. Almost at once, they revealed the walls of a buried city. The men dug down and down, and the deeper they went, the older the ruins were. By 1873, Schliemann was almost at the foot of the mound, and then, on May 31, he saw the glint of gold in the side of a trench. He sent the workers for an early break so they would not see what he had found. Then, in great secrecy, Schliemann pulled gold and silver objects and stunning jewelry from the ground. He later claimed he passed them to his wife, Sophia, who hid them in her shawl—but he made this story up. But Schliemann did smuggle the treasure out of Turkey. First he moved it to Athens, Greece, and finally to Berlin, Germany, where it was displayed in a museum.

◀ This gold jewelry found by Schliemann at Troy is part of a hoard that became known as the Jewels of Helen. Schliemann believed it belonged to Helen of Troy, an important figure in Homer's story.

FACT FILE

Schliemann tried to sell the Trojan treasure to the British Museum, London, for £50,000 (around $32,500), but he was turned down.

LOST:
THE FAMILY SILVER

In CE 43, the Roman army invaded Britain, and soon all of Wales and most of England were under Roman command. However, by the 300s, invaders were challenging the Romans for control of Britain. It was a difficult time for the people who lived there.

Location: Near Mildenhall, Britain
Date: 4th century CE

The trouble began when Saxon raiders from Germany came to the east coast of Britain. The Romans tried to stop them. Britain was their property, and they were not about to give it up without a fight, so they built a line of forts along the coast. But these defenses were too little, too late.

▼ About 1,700 years ago, a distressed family buried a hoard of silver in a field in eastern England. They hoped to dig it up when the danger had passed—but something prevented them from returning.

The Children's Spoons

Among the pieces buried were two silver spoons engraved with the Roman girls' names Papittedo and Pascentia. These were probably the names of the daughters of the family. Spoons such as these were common christening gifts for Christian children born into Roman families.

As the Saxon raids continued, people must have wondered what was going to happen to them. Most people thought of themselves as sophisticated Romans, and were afraid of the Saxon **barbarians**. For one family, panic seems to have set in. We do not know the family's name, but we do know they lived near what is now the town of Mildenhall in Suffolk, possibly in a grand **villa**. They were wealthy, perhaps one of the richest Roman families in Britain. One day they gathered up their valuables—dishes, bowls, spoons, ladles, and goblets, all made of the finest silver—and buried them in a nearby field.

The family probably intended to recover their valuables once the danger of the barbarian raiders had passed, but they never did. They vanished without trace, leaving the family silver for others to find.

▼ This Roman fort at Portchester, near Portsmouth, is one of the many forts built by the Romans around the southern English coast. Portchester fort was intended to guard the harbor at Portsmouth from the Saxon raiders.

FOUND:
THE MILDENHALL TREASURE

Entombed in the underground darkness, the pieces of Roman silver waited for the day when they would come back into the light. It was a long wait. For 1,600 years, the Mildenhall soil guarded its secret well. And then, in January 1942, the silver was revealed by a plow.

Farmhand Gordon Butcher drove his tractor back and forth across the field, his plow biting deep into the ground. It was a freezing winter's day and snow settled in the plow furrows, making white stripes in the dark earth. Then the plow hit something hard, and Mr. Butcher climbed down from the tractor to investigate.

▼ This silver bowl has a decorated, dome-shaped cover. It is adorned with wild beasts and centaurs—part horse, part human creature—from mythology.

FACT FILE

The Mildenhall Treasure was found only because Gordon Butcher's plow happened to go deeper into the ground than usual.

There, in the furrow, was a piece of metal. It was not at all like the twisted scraps he usually found. His boss, Sydney Ford, joined him, and between them they pulled 34 blackened plates, bowls, spoons, and cups from the ground. Mr. Ford, who was interested in old things, took the pieces home, and he cleaned and polished them one by one until the silver was as shiny as new. He displayed them on his sideboard. He used one dish as a fruit bowl, and even ate his oatmeal with one of the silver spoons.

In 1946, four years after it was found, the silver plowed up in a Suffolk field was handed over to the British Museum, London. Ever since, it has been known as the Mildenhall Treasure—one of the greatest finds of Roman silver ever made.

Unlikely Treasure Divided Experts

When the Mildenhall Treasure was first displayed in the British Museum, some experts thought it was fake. They could not believe that such good-quality, highly decorated silverware could be Roman. They were also suspicious because of the strange circumstances of its discovery. However, experts are now agreed that the treasure is genuine and was produced in the 4th century CE by Roman craftspeople.

▲ The face of the sea god Neptune stares out from the center of the Great Dish—the most important piece in the Mildenhall Treasure. Neptune has a seaweed beard and four dolphins swim around him.

LOST: A LIBRARY OF SCROLLS

About 2,000 years ago, a group of men lived at Qumran, a remote place on the shore of the Dead Sea, in the Roman province of Judea. They were the Essenes—deeply religious Jews who had chosen to live in the wilderness, far away from Jerusalem and the rest of the world.

Location: Qumran, West Bank (Palestine)
Date: CE 66–70

The Essenes spent their days praying, taking part in ceremonies and performing rituals, and studying. Inside a special building called a **scriptorium**, they created a library. Word for word, men copied out old holy texts onto rolls of **parchment** and **papyrus** called **scrolls**. Some of the texts they copied were hundreds of years old. Copying by hand was the only way of making new texts for future generations to read. The scrolls were the Essenes' most precious possessions, and they would do anything to protect them.

▶ The scriptorium was the most important building for the community at Qumran.

▲ The caves at Qumran are hollowed out from the soft limestone. The Essenes may have carved out some of the caves themselves, to store things in or to live in.

In CE 66, a rebellion began, started by Jews who wanted to throw the Romans off their land. The Jews were defeated and the Romans took their revenge. They destroyed Jerusalem, and in about CE 70 they attacked Qumran. The Essenes gathered up their precious scrolls, wrapped them in linen, packed them into clay jars, and headed to nearby cliffs. They climbed nearly vertical walls to caves high above the ground, where they hid their library of scrolls. After this, the Essenes vanished, and no one knows what happened to them. As for their scrolls, the Essenes had found the perfect hiding place.

Storing the Scrolls

The Essenes rolled up their scrolls and put them inside clay jars, like this one. They hid the jars inside caves high up in the cliffs, and there they stayed for 2,000 years. The dry desert climate kept them from decomposing. The texts the Essenes copied were all holy books, including many from the Hebrew Bible (the Old Testament in the Christian Bible). They wrote in three languages: Hebrew, Aramaic, and Greek.

LOST:
ROMAN VILLA

The towns around the Bay of Naples, Italy, were home to thousands of Romans. In between the towns were farms, and the grand country houses, or villas, of the rich. For the owner of the Villa Pisanella on the slopes of the hill called Vesuvius, life was good.

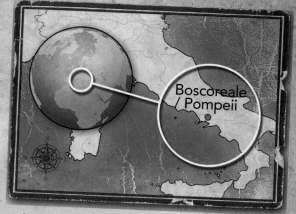

Location: Boscoreale, near Pompeii, Italy
Date: August 24, CE 79

The villa was the home of Lucius Iucundus, a wealthy banker from nearby Pompeii. It was where he went to relax with his family, a place of peace and quiet away from the noise and crowds in the city where he had made his fortune. He had slaves to tend his vineyards, and there was a press to squeeze the grapes into wine.

In one terrifying day, the world of Lucius Iucundus, and of thousands of people like him, was suddenly ended. The volcano of Vesuvius erupted violently, spewing out fire, ash, and rock. The towns around the bay were destroyed and many people in them were killed. About 2,000 people died in Pompeii alone.

▼ This wall painting, or fresco, shows a grand Roman house much like the Villa Pisanella. Pillars support the roof, and frescoes decorate the walls.

Pompeii, the Town That Died

Pompeii was around 5 miles (8 kilometers) south of Vesuvius. When the volcano erupted, the wind blew ash and rock into the town. It piled up in the streets and on the roofs. Thousands of people fled from their homes. The end came when three great flows of volcanic debris rushed down from the volcano and completely covered the buildings. The people still in the town died, and Pompeii vanished.

At the Villa Pisanella, a woman had hidden in the cellar, hoping to escape the choking fumes and ash. In there with her were 109 pieces of fine silver tableware and 1,037 gold coins. She may have been a member of the family, or perhaps a slave. Whoever she was, the cellar became her tomb as the villa disappeared beneath a layer of volcanic ash. From that day on, the silver and gold were buried treasure.

▼ The volcano filled the air with poisonous fumes. It became impossible to breathe, and the woman hiding in the cellar would have choked to death.

FOUND:

THE BOSCOREALE TREASURE

In 1868, workmen were digging at Boscoreale, near the ancient Roman town of Pompeii. They came across walls and mosaic floors, and realized they had found the remains of a Roman villa destroyed in the eruption of Vesuvius.

The dig had to stop because the landowner next door refused to give permission for her land to be excavated. But when the landowner died the dig started again and, by 1895, the whole of the villa had been uncovered. Living rooms, servants' quarters, bathrooms, a kitchen, a bakery, and rooms for pressing grapes were uncovered. In one room, tools were found still hanging on the wall—as if the occupants had just left the house, rather than 1,800 years earlier.

▲ A bracelet and ring found at Boscoreale, probably owned by the woman of the house.

FACT FILE

Boscoreale was a wealthy area with lots of fancy villas and a special hunting preserve.

▼ Workers excavate Pompeii in 1895. Excavations began in 1748 an archeologists are still uncovering th city's hidden secrets.

▼ Gold jewelry, such as these pieces from Boscoreale, would have been kept in the family by passing from mother to daughter.

When the archeologists dug into the cellar, they made the find of a lifetime. Out of the ash came a hoard of 109 silver plates, bowls, jugs, and cups. It was a complete Roman dinner service, fit to grace the table at the grandest of banquets. Scattered around it were gold coins, and nearby were the bones of a woman who had died in the disaster.

The Boscoreale Treasure had been safe for all the years it lay buried. But, once it was out of the ground, dealers, private collectors, and museums were all fighting over it. The treasure was split up, and today it is in museums around the world.

This silver mirror (left), found at Boscoreale, has a highly polished surface for reflecting. The silver bowl (above) may have been used to pour special drinks during religious ceremonies.

Skeleton Cup

Among the Boscoreale Treasure were two silver wine cups decorated with pictures of human skeletons. To modern eyes, the scenes seem macabre or even scary, but not to the Romans. To them, these cups were a way of saying "drink up and make the most of today, before it's too late and you become a skeleton!" Today, the famous skeleton cups are in the Louvre Museum, Paris, France.

LOST:
GOLD IN THE LAKE

In the mountains of Colombia, South America, lies Lake Guatavita. The lake was sacred to the Muisca people. They believed two things about it: first, that a terrible goddess lived in the waters; second, that it was their duty to shower the goddess with gifts.

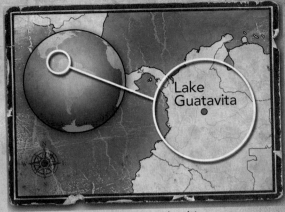

Location: Lake Guatavita, Colombia
Date: 1500s

The gift-giving ceremony took place whenever a new king was chosen. It was his first job, and one of his most spectacular duties. He was sent to a cave, where he spent a few days on his own. He was forbidden to eat salt or chili pepper to purify his body, and he was not allowed to leave the cave during the hours of daylight. In this way he prepared himself for an unforgettable journey.

▲ Lake Guatavita is an almost perfect circle. It sits inside a steep-sided hollow, possibly a crater made by a meterorite crashing into the Earth. Today, the lake is about 120 feet (37 meters) deep. The V-shaped notch was cut by Spanish invaders in 1578, when they tried to drain the lake in search of gold.

The Gold Raft

This gold model shows the king and his chiefs on the raft that floated across Lake Guatavita. Coated in gold dust, the king jumped into the water from the raft. He was allowed to return to the shore only after the specks of gold had all washed off. Then worshippers threw gold offerings into the lake. This ceremony was designed to please the goddess of the lake who, the Muisca people believed, loved gold more than anything.

When the time came, servants took the king to Lake Guatavita. They stripped him naked, and smeared his body with mud. They blew gold dust over him. It stuck to the mud, covering him from head to toe and transforming him into a golden man. He took his place on a raft made from rushes, and four of his chiefs joined him. The sweet smell of burning incense filled the air, sending a signal to the gods that the king was coming. The raft floated to the center of the lake, where the king and his chiefs threw handfuls of gold objects and emeralds into the water.

Over the years, countless thousands of precious objects were cast into Lake Guatavita as offerings to Chie, the Muisca goddess of water. They sank to the bottom of the lake. The Muisca thought no more of them, but not all people were like them. In time, treasure hunters came in search of the gold in the lake.

▼ Attendants blew gold dust through reed pipes onto the king's body, to turn him into a "golden man."

27

FOUND:

THE GOLD OF EL DORADO

In the 1530s, explorers from Spain arrived in Colombia in search of gold. They heard stories about a golden man who ruled a mountain kingdom where gold was commonplace. They named the mysterious kingdom El Dorado (the golden one), and they were determined to find it.

▲ This figure of a warrior god is made from pure gold. In one hand he holds an enemy's head, and in the other a knife.

The story that a golden kingdom was waiting to be discovered captured the imaginations of treasure hunters, and led to the longest treasure hunt in history. In 1539, Spanish soldiers reached Lake Guatavita. They looted gold from the villages, then left, thinking the golden kingdom must be elsewhere. But stories about gold at the bottom of the lake soon drew them back. In the 1540s, treasure hunters forced local people to lower the lake's water level. Day after day they carried away buckets of water, until the muddy edges of the lake could be searched. Disappointingly, only a few pieces of gold were found. The most dramatic attempt at draining the lake came in 1578, when a gigantic notch was cut into its side. As the water drained out, some gold objects were revealed but it was not the haul the treasure hunters had hoped for. Was the treasure still hidden, at the center of the lake?

The search of Lake Guatavita continued until, in 1965, the Colombian government banned further searches. And so the story ends, perhaps with untold riches still out of reach at the bottom of Lake Guatavita.

Precious Metal

To the Muisca people of Colombia, the Incas of Peru, and the Aztecs of Mexico, gold was a useful metal from which they could make sacred objects, such as this figure. To the Spanish invaders, gold meant wealth. They were determined to get their hands on as much as they could, even if that meant becoming **looters**.

FACT FILE

Experts have estimated that half a million offerings were thrown into Lake Guatavita. No one knows how many are still in the lake.

▼ In vain Spanish soldiers searched South America for a golden kingdom they called El Dorado.

▼ This gold object was worn on a person's forehead. The two large circles are meant to represent the eyes of a big jungle cat.

TIMELINE
OF DISCOVERIES

1868
At Hildesheim, Germany, a hoard of Roman silver bowls and cups is discovered.

1873
Gold treasure found at Troy, Turkey.

1895
At Boscoreale, near Pompeii, Italy, a hoard of Roman gold and silver is found.

1922
The tomb and treasures of pharaoh Tutankhamun are uncovered in Egypt.

1927
Royal graves containing great treasures are found at Ur, Iraq.

1939
An Anglo-Saxon treasure is found at Sutton Hoo, England.

1942
The Mildenhall Treasure of Roman silver is discovered in England.

1946–47
The Dead Sea Scrolls are found in caves at Qumran, West Bank (Palestine).

1972
A diver finds two ancient Greek bronze statues on the seabed off the coast of Riace, Italy.

1974
Farmers in China dig up pieces of pottery and bronze, leading to the discovery of the Terracotta Army.

1985
A vast haul of gold and silver from the Middle Ages is found in Poland. It becomes known as the Šroda Treasure.

1986
At Rogozen, Bulgaria, 165 pieces of silver treasure from the ancient kingdom of Thrace are found.

1987
At Sipán, Peru, an ancient burial mound is opened, and a royal treasure found.

1992
The Hoxne Hoard of Roman gold and silver is found in England.

2009
A metal-detector user in England finds the Staffordshire Hoard of Anglo-Saxon treasure.

GLOSSARY

archeologist
A person who digs up and studies the remains of the past.

barbarian
An uncivilized person.

BCE
Used in dates. Means "Before the Common Era." The Common Era begins with year 1.

bronze
A yellowish metal made from a mixture of copper and tin.

burial mound
A hill made of earth built over the burial place of a dead person.

CE
Used in dates. Means "Common Era." The Common Era begins with year 1 which is the same as the year AD 1 in the Christian calendar.

empire
A group of lands or countries ruled by one person or government.

hoard
A large number of items saved by their owner, often by burying them in the ground.

looter
Someone who steals valuable items from a defeated enemy, after a battle, or from an archeological site.

mercury
A silvery metal which is a liquid, not a solid.

mud brick
A building brick made from clay, often mixed with chopped straw or grass, and dried hard by the sun.

papyrus
A type of writing paper made from the stem of a water reed.

parchment
A type of writing paper made from the skins of animals.

scriptorium
A place where books were copied out by hand to make new copies of them.

scroll
A roll of paper or parchment.

terracotta
Items of brownish-red pottery which have been baked hard in an oven.

treasure hunter
A person who searches for treasure. Some treasure hunters damage ancient sites; others work with archeologists.

villa
A country house in ancient Rome or its provinces.

INDEX